HEALTH CHOICES

HARMFUL SUBSTANCES

Cath Senker

HODDER
Wayland

An imprint of Hodder Children's Books

Text copyright © Cath Senker 2004

Consultant: Jayne Wright
Design: Sarah Borny

Published in Great Britain in 2004
by Hodder Wayland, an imprint of
Hodder Children's Books

The publishers would like to thank the following for allowing
us to reproduce their pictures in this book:
Corbis; 6, 8, 11, 12 / Hodder Wayland Picture Library; 7, 9, 14
15, 16, 17, 19, 20, 21 / Zul Mukhida 4, 5, 13, 18

A catalogue record for this book is available from the British Library.

ISBN 07502 44992

Printed in China by WKT

Hodder Children's Books
A division of Hodder Headline Limited
338 Euston Road, London NW1 3BH

Contents

What are drugs?

 A drug is something that changes the way your body works. It makes you feel different.

Medicines are drugs that can make you better if you are ill. They can kill germs and stop a pain from hurting. Medicines can stop you from getting nasty diseases.

It is important to choose the right kind of medicine.

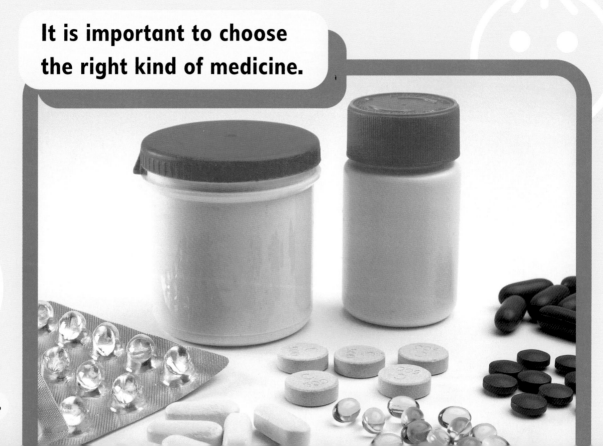

When were you last ill? Did you need medicine or did you get better by yourself?

If you take the wrong drug, or you take too much, it can harm you. You might become sleepy, spotty or really sick.

Alcohol and cigarettes are also drugs. They can make people ill. Some people use powerful drugs that are against the law. They can be very dangerous too.

I feel ill. What can I do?

We all get coughs and colds, sore throats and tummy aches. Usually your body gets better all by itself.

Do you need a drug for a bug? Sometimes you need some medicine to help you get better. There are no cures for colds and flu but medicine can make you feel more comfortable.

An adult

can buy you

medicines for

coughs and

colds, or aches

and pains. They can

be bought from a chemist,

general store or supermarket. The packet tells you the

dose you should take. Soon you will feel well again.

Where should medicines be kept at home?

(Answer on page 23)

Why do I need to take medicine?

Feeling ill and need a pill? Sometimes you have something wrong with you that won't get better by itself. Perhaps the person looking after you doesn't know what is making you ill.

If you're really sick, go to the doctor quick! The doctor will see what is wrong. You might need a special medicine. The doctor will write a note called a **prescription**. An adult will take it to the chemist to get the right medicine.

Medicines can come as liquids, tablets, or creams. Some are injected or sniffed up the nose.

Use your medicine just as the doctor says. Too little and you won't get better. Too much and you might get more ill.

Why should you never take a medicine that is for someone else?

(Answer on page 23)

What are herbal medicines?

 Not all medicines come from the doctor. Some people go to health food shops. They can buy medicines made from herbs and other plants. People should take care with them, just like with all medicines.

To get advice you can go to see a herbalist. The **herbalist** knows about using herbs as medicines. People may choose to visit a **homeopath**. Homeopaths use different kinds of medicines from the ones doctors use.

Do you know anyone who uses herbal or homeopathic medicines? Have you used them yourself and did they help?

A herbalist chooses the right herbs to help make you better.

Many different plants are used in herbal medicine.

Why do I need injections?

When you were little you probably had some injections.

What have you had injections for?
(Answer on page 23)

The doctor uses a small needle that goes under your skin. This tiny little pinprick can stop you getting sick.

Injections help to stop you catching diseases and keep you healthy.

The needle contains a drug. It can protect you from nasty diseases like **measles**, **mumps** or **TB**. It works like this. The measles drug contains a very weak kind of measles. Your body kills the measles easily. If you're ever close to people with the real disease, your body already knows how to fight it off.

Why has my friend got an inhaler?

Some people have conditions that can make them ill. Many children have **asthma**. It can make breathing difficult. They need to use an **inhaler** (puffer). It has a drug in it to help them to breathe easily.

Some children take tablets to control **epilepsy**. Children with **diabetes** need to inject themselves with a special drug called insulin.

They learn to do the injections on their own.

Do you or your friends need to take special medicines?

Remember! When you are prescribed a drug, it is for you alone. Never use someone else's medicine, even if you have the same condition or illness.

Household chemicals do a useful job. Cleaning fluids are needed to make your home clean and fresh. Have you ever broken a favourite toy? An adult probably used strong glue to mend it.

This symbol is on dangerous chemicals so that you know they could be harmful.

Household chemicals are very powerful. They can harm you if you don't use them in the right way. Strong cleaners like bleach could make you very sick if you swallowed them by accident. Some kinds of glue have a strong smell. It makes you feel quite unwell.

Which household chemicals do you have at home? Learn to keep away from them. Look after yourself – leave chemicals on the shelf!

Why do people drink alcohol?

 Many adults drink alcohol because it helps them to feel more lively or relaxed.

Alcohol is a powerful drug. People should think before they drink. If they drink too much, they will get drunk. Drunk people can be noisy and frightening. They may not know what they are doing. They can cause accidents.

Do you know which drinks have alcohol in them?

(Answer on page 23)

**Go for healthy drinks like milk or juice.
This girl is enjoying a delicious milkshake.**

Alcohol is too strong for children's small bodies. It can

make them drunk very quickly. Some alcoholic drinks

have fruit in them and look like they are for children.

Beware – these drinks could be harmful.

Why is smoking so bad for you?

 Many people smoke. They say it helps them to relax and feels good.

But smoking makes people smell – and their clothes as well. It makes them ill. The chemicals in cigarette smoke are poisonous. They go into the smoker's body and damage the lungs. It can then become hard for them to breathe.

What would you do if someone offered you a cigarette?

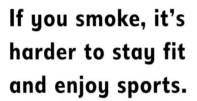

If you smoke, it's harder to stay fit and enjoy sports.

Smoking makes people's bodies need more cigarettes. They become *addicted*. They find it hard to stop smoking even if they want to. It's best not to start smoking in the first place.

If people around you smoke, you breathe in the dangerous chemicals too. This is bad for your health.

Glossary and index

measles 13   A disease that gives you fever and small red spots all over the body.

mumps 13   A disease that makes the sides of your face swell up.

prescription 8   A piece of paper on which the doctor writes down the medicine you need.

TB (Tuberculosis) 13   A serious disease that causes swellings on the lungs and other parts of the body.

Answers to questions:

P.7 Medicines should be kept in a locked cabinet, out of the reach of children.

P.9 If you take a medicine that is for someone else it could be dangerous for you. All people are different and the medicines they need are often different too.

P.12 Children in the UK usually have injections against diphtheria, tetanus, whooping cough, polio, meningitis, measles, mumps and rubella.

P.18 These are some drinks that have alcohol in them: beer, wine, whisky, vodka, gin, alcopops.

Finding out more

Books to read:
Drugs and Your Health
by Jillian Powell
(Hodder Wayland, 2002)

Nice or Nasty? Learning About Drugs and Your Health
by Claire Llewellyn and Mike Gordon
(Hodder Wayland, 1999)

The Nosmo King
by Phyllis Abbott
(1st Books Library, 2001)

What About Health; Drugs
by Fiona Waters
(Hodder Wayland, 2001)

What do we Think About Alcohol?
by Jen Green
(Hodder Wayland, 2001)